Strong Girls in History

STRONG GIRLS
in History

★ **15 YOUNG ACHIEVERS YOU SHOULD KNOW** ★

Susan B. Katz

Illustrations by Monika Róża Wiśniewska

ROCKRIDGE
PRESS

First Rockridge Press trade paperback edition 2022

Rockridge Press and the Rockridge Press logo are trademarks or registered trademarks of Callisto Media Inc. and/or its affiliates in the United States and other countries and may not be used without written permission.

For general information on our other products and services, please contact our Customer Care Department within the United States at (866) 744-2665, or outside the United States at (510) 253-0500.

Some of the biographies in this book originally appeared, in different form, in *Strong Girls in History* by Susan B. Katz.

Paperback ISBN: 978-1-68539-502-5 | eBook ISBN: 978-1-63878-012-0

Manufactured in the United States of America

Series Designer: Will Mack
Interior and Cover Designer: Jane Archer
Art Producer: Samantha Ulban
Editor: Barbara J. Isenberg
Production Editor: Rachel Taenzler
Production Manager: David Zapanta

Illustrations © 2021 Monika Róża Wiśniewska. Author photo courtesy of Jeanne Marquis Photography.

10 9 8 7 6 5 4 3 2 1 0

*To all the strong girls
I've taught over the years: some are
aspiring Olympians now,
others are acting, a few are
scientists and doctors.
Very proud of you all!*

Contents

Introduction

What do Amanda Gorman, Greta Thunberg, and Malala Yousafzai have in common? They are all strong women! Women throughout history have changed the world in many important ways. They have stood up to unfair laws, won record numbers of Olympic medals, and worked to cure cancer. This should come as no surprise. Girls and women are powerful, smart, and determined. Inside these pages are the stories of 15 girls who made an impact before they were 20 years old. Each strong girl worked hard, overcame obstacles, and changed the world.

Strength comes in all shapes and sizes. The girls in this book are proof that no matter who you are, where you're from, or what you look like, you can achieve great things. They come from all corners of the world, practice different religions, and speak diverse languages. They've set the bar sky-high for what it means to be a real-life superhero.

You will first read about Audrey Faye Hendricks, one of the youngest people to be arrested while protesting unfair laws against Black people. Then you will meet the author of *The Outsiders*, S. E. Hinton, a ballerina named Yuan Yuan Tan, and more recent heroes like Malala Yousafzai, who fought for girls to be able to go to school in Pakistan. We can learn things from each one of their lives. Most of them, like Simone Biles, faced challenges but overcame them and accomplished things no girl before them ever had.

Each of the strong girls featured in this book was chosen because she did something special in an area like art, sports, politics, writing, or music. Their achievements were groundbreaking, and they had to overcome many barriers or challenges.

This book will explore who these girls were, where they were from, and when they lived. You'll learn about their work, the challenges they faced, and what impact they've had on the world. If the person has passed, we will talk about her legacy and how it's important today. If she is living, we will highlight how she is still making an impact on the world.

When you are finished reading this book, I hope you'll understand more about what it means to be a strong girl and come away motivated to make a difference in the world. The future is female!

Audrey Faye
HENDRICKS

1953–2009

Audrey Hendricks was the youngest person ever to be arrested for protesting **segregation**, as part of the Children's Crusade. She was nine. Later on in life, she was part of the first class of students to integrate the local high school, meaning Black and white students attended together.

Audrey Faye Hendricks was born in Birmingham, Alabama, in 1953. Joe, Audrey's father, and Lola, her mother, both actively fought for the rights of Black people in their city. In fact, her dad was arrested, along with 15 other Black men, because they wouldn't give up their seats on a bus to white people. It was illegal at the time for Black people to sit on the bus if white people wanted seats. They all spent six nights in jail. Her mother organized protests and **boycotts** in Birmingham. Many of her uncles also fought for **civil rights**. It made sense that Audrey would grow up wanting to fight for Black people's rights, too!

In the 19th and 20th centuries, Jim Crow laws prevented Black people from being in the same places as white people in areas like schools, swimming pools, and bathrooms. Even after the Supreme Court ruled that segregation was **unconstitutional**, Birmingham kept on segregating buses, restaurants, and schools.

Birmingham was a city full of racial violence. Black churches were bombed and Black people were attacked on the streets. The police commissioner, Bull Connor, was famous for his support of segregation and his use of violence to enforce it. Audrey's parents and other civil rights **activists** sued the city for remaining segregated. In 1961, they won the lawsuit to **desegregate** the 67 public parks in Birmingham. Bull Connor was furious and closed all the parks to get back at them.

Every Monday, Audrey and her family went to meetings at a local church. These meetings were put together by the Alabama Christian Movement for Human Rights (ACMHR). The group was started by a pastor and family friend, Reverend Fred Shuttlesworth. Some days, Audrey and other children attended special ACMHR meetings. Audrey said, "[There] was no way for me not to really be involved. . . . My parents were involved from the point that I could remember. . . . My church was involved. . . . You were there and just a part of it."

In 1963, Reverend Shuttlesworth asked Dr. Martin Luther King Jr. to help with the situation in Birmingham. Dr. King was an important civil rights leader. He agreed to help desegregate Birmingham.

Marching, demonstrating, or protesting against segregation was illegal, so many activists were put in jail. Many adults were afraid of getting arrested because they didn't want to lose their jobs. During one of Dr. King's speeches at Audrey's church, he encouraged everybody, young and old, to join in the effort to gain equality, even if it meant getting arrested. "Fill the jails!" he said. Dr. King's words inspired young Audrey. The night after he spoke at her church, Audrey went home and told her parents, "I want to get arrested." Her parents were proud of her for wanting to be involved in this important cause.

> **"I DO REMEMBER GOING TO TELL MY TEACHER THAT I WAS GOING TO MARCH AND GET ARRESTED AND SHE CRIED. I THINK BECAUSE SHE WAS SO TOUCHED."**

On May 2, 1963, nine-year-old Audrey and thousands of other children walked down the steps of the 16th Street Baptist Church while singing "Ain't Gonna Let Nobody Turn Me Around." This event was called the Children's Crusade. As they marched, the children were attacked by police dogs and sprayed with fire hoses before getting arrested. The jails became so full of children that the police used a fairgrounds as a holding place.

When Audrey was arrested, her parents watched proudly as their daughter was put into the police car. In jail, Audrey was forced to share a bathroom with several dozen girls. "I didn't have any fresh underwear, a change of clothes, or a toothbrush," Audrey said. She couldn't see, or talk to, her parents for almost seven days!

The 500 children who were arrested were released from jail on Wednesday, May 8. Audrey went back to school the next day as if it were no big deal. None of her friends even asked her about being in jail. She was the only student from her school to go to the protest.

After the Crusade, the newspapers printed pictures of children being fire-hosed with water and attacked by police dogs. Those pictures made people around the country angry. They forced the government to do something to stop the violence against children. White city leaders sat down with Black civil rights activists. They agreed to end segregation in Birmingham. Audrey and the other children of the Crusade had successfully forced white leaders to end segregation in their city!

When she was older, Audrey asked to be one of the students in the first integrated class at the high school, meaning Black and white kids would be in the same school. She started attending the class 15 years after the Supreme Court passed *Brown v. Board of Education*—the legal decision that had desegrated schools in the United States. For the first two weeks, all the Black students sat in the auditorium because the school didn't know what to do with them.

Audrey eventually went to college in Dallas, Texas, and worked there for four years after graduating. Then she moved back to her hometown of Birmingham. When she returned, Audrey taught young kids from underserved (or struggling) families for 25 years. She earned a master's degree in 2007. Her thesis, or final paper, focused on women who fought in the Civil Rights Movement.

Audrey's bravery and determination helped Black people gain equality in Birmingham and throughout the United States. At a very young age, she felt like it was her responsibility to take part in the Children's Crusade. That march in Birmingham helped tip the scales so that desegregation was finally law in her hometown. In high school, she volunteered to be among the first Black students to integrate. Audrey will always be remembered for building bridges between Black people and white people and fighting for what she believed in.

EXPLORE MORE! Read more about the Children's Crusade in Birmingham in *We've Got a Job: The 1963 Birmingham Children's March* by Cynthia Levinson.

DID YOU KNOW? During Christmastime one year, white people from other states sent hundreds of presents to the children of Birmingham. Audrey remembers the gifts arriving at her house. The gifts meant a lot to her and her family.

S. E. HINTON

1948–present

When she was a teenager, Susie Hinton published a novel called *The Outsiders*. At just 15 years old, she wrote a book that reflected her real-life high school experiences. Her book was so popular that it became a famous movie! Susie Hinton's books launched a new type of writing (a *genre*) called Young Adult. Her books are written especially for readers between the ages of 12 and 18.

Susan (Susie) Eloise Hinton was born on July 22, 1948 in Tulsa, Oklahoma. Susie was always shy, and she loved horseback riding. There wasn't a lot to do in Tulsa. Other than riding horses, Susie loved to read. Though she thought she might grow up to be a cattle rancher, her love of reading and writing became her passion.

Susie enjoyed books by great writers like F. Scott Fitzgerald, Jane Austen, and Mary Renault. When her father got cancer, Susie dove into writing to help her cope with that difficult time. Most of her early stories were about horses and cowboys. Susie noticed, though, that she couldn't find many books about what was going on in her life. So, she began to write about what it is really like to be a teenager.

Susie went to Will Rogers High School. At the time, the school had two **rival** gangs who fought a lot: the Greasers and the Socs. The Greasers were poorer students, and the Socs (which stood for "Socials") were the wealthier kids. Susie didn't see any books that showed what being in a gang was like. After one of her friends was beaten up, Susie decided to write a book from the point of view of one of the Greasers.

In 1967, Susie sold her story to a big publisher two years after writing it. When her book, *The Outsiders*, came out that year, she used the **pen name** S. E. Hinton. Her editor thought boys would not read her book if they knew it was written by a woman. By using her initials, she made sure that nobody knew her gender.

The Outsiders is about friendship and **loyalty**. It shows how similar the boys in the two gangs really are. The main character is named Ponyboy, a 14-year-old Greaser who is an orphan. Ponyboy faces the deaths of people he loves, and he learns that he doesn't have to be an outsider. The book was a huge success! Kids could see themselves in Susie's book.

> **"THE REST OF MY BOOKS I WROTE, BUT *THE OUTSIDERS* WAS MEANT TO BE WRITTEN. I GOT CHOSEN TO WRITE IT."**

Soon, S. E. Hinton became famous. Her book was so popular that it sold more than four million copies in the United States alone! Susie was able to use the money from book sales to pay for college at the University of Tulsa. She graduated in 1970 with a degree in education. She also met her future husband, David Inhofe, there.

At age 18, Susie became known as "The Voice of the Youth." But fame and fortune put her under a lot of pressure. Susie felt so stressed that she developed something called "writer's block." She didn't write another book for three years!

Susie was sad and stuck, and David didn't like seeing her like that. So, he said that she had to write two pages every day if she wanted to leave the house. David's idea gave her the motivation she needed. Susie's next novel, *That Was Then, This Is Now*, came out in 1971. It was about two best friends, Bryon and Mark, whose bond begins to come apart as they grow up.

Her 1975 novel, *Rumble Fish*, was adapted from a short story she had written earlier. One reviewer said it was her best book so far, while another said it would be her last. But that reviewer was very wrong! Four years later, Susie's book *Tex* told the story of two brothers left to take care of themselves while their father is away for months at a time. When the movie adaptation came out in 1982, Susie actually made a **cameo** appearance in it!

Susie Hinton's books were so popular that her teen readers begged for them to be made into movies. In 1983, *The Outsiders* movie made $5 million on its opening weekend. It has since grossed $25 million! Susie spent months on the film set, advising the actors and famous director Francis Ford Coppola. Later, she worked with Coppola to co-write the **screenplay** for *Rumble Fish*.

Two months before the *Rumble Fish* movie came out in 1983, Susie and David had a son named Nicholas. In 1985, the movie version of *That Was Then, This Is Now* was released.

It took Susie years to write her next novel, *Taming the Star Runner*, which was published in 1988. Many readers believe that the main character, Travis, is based on Susie's own experience as a teenage writer. Unlike her other books, *Taming the Star Runner* is written in third-person voice. All her other books are in first-person.

Susie has won numerous awards for her books. In 1988, she received the very first Margaret A. Edwards Award from the American Library Association and *School Library Journal*. S. E. later wrote two books for little kids called *Big David, Little David* and *The Puppy Sister*.

Some people were upset that *The Outsiders* showed gang behavior and that her books dealt with material some adults thought was inappropriate. Others even banned her books. But millions of readers keep asking for them at libraries and in schools.

Susie basically invented the Young Adult, or "YA," genre. Before Susie, there were very few books for teen-agers and young adults. Her books are now classics, taught in schools all over the world.

When Susie saw that there weren't books showing what real life was like for teens, she wanted to change that. It all began with *The Outsiders*. That book has since sold more than 15 million copies and been translated into 30 languages! It didn't just make her famous—it introduced a whole new genre of books for teens.

EXPLORE MORE! To learn more about important thinkers like Susie Hinton, check out *Leaders and Thinkers in American History: 15 Influential People You Should Know* by Megan DuVarney Forbes.

DID YOU KNOW? Susie Hinton writes all her books by putting pen to paper. Then, she types her books on a computer. Her first **royalty** check was for $10, but now she's worth $10 million!

Yuan Yuan
TAN
1976–present

B allet dancer Yuan Yuan Tan became the youngest principal dancer (the highest-level dancer) in the San Francisco Ballet company at age 19. Twenty-five years later, she still dances with the company—longer than any other principal dancer in its history. She also was featured on the cover of *Time* magazine—something no other ballet dancer from China has achieved.

Yuan Yuan Tan was born in Shanghai, China, on February 14, 1976. She was very active as a child and liked climbing trees and being outdoors. But what Yuan Yuan liked to do most was dance. When she saw a performance of *Swan Lake* on TV, she fell in love with ballet. She knew that she wanted to go to dance school to become a ballet dancer.

Yuan Yuan's father wanted her to become a doctor, not a dancer, but her mother was very supportive of her dancing. Yuan Yuan's mom had wanted to be a dancer herself, but her father (Yuan Yuan's grandfather) wouldn't allow it. In a way, Yuan Yuan was fulfilling her mother's dream. To decide whether or not she could dance, her family flipped a coin! The coin landed on heads and Yuan Yuan started attending the Shanghai Ballet dance school when she was 11 years old. She moved away to live near the school.

Learning ballet wasn't easy. At first, Yuan Yuan's teachers told her that she looked more like a soft noodle than a strong ballet dancer. She was homesick and thought about leaving the school. But Yuan Yuan was determined to get better and train harder.

Her hard work paid off. When she was only 16, Yuan Yuan earned a gold medal at the 5th International Ballet Competition in Paris, France. The following year, she won the Nijinsky Award and another gold medal at the 1st Japan International Ballet and Modern Dance Competition. People were starting to notice the graceful ballerina from China.

> **"I'M A PRETTY SHY PERSON, USUALLY. I'M GRATEFUL THAT EVERYBODY WILL BE THERE, BUT I DON'T ASK FOR ANY ATTENTION."**

In February 1995, Yuan Yuan was attending dance school in Germany when Helgi Tomasson, the artistic director of the San Francisco Ballet, approached her. He asked Yuan Yuan to stop in San Francisco and dance as a guest artist for one night. She agreed, thinking that her first dance with the San Francisco Ballet would be her last. When she finished performing, Yuan Yuan went to Tomasson's office and said the only two words of English that she knew at the time: "Thank you." That day changed her life!

After watching her performance, Tomasson knew Yuan Yuan was someone special. He told her that he wanted her to stay with the San Francisco Ballet company. He told Yuan Yuan that she could be a soloist right away. He also told her she didn't have to start as a lower-ranking dancer like most other new dancers did.

Yuan Yuan had a hard decision to make. She was on a scholarship at the dance school in Germany and planned to dance with the Stuttgart Ballet. She had already started learning German. The thought of learning another language overwhelmed her. Not sure what to do, Yuan Yuan took a bus to San Francisco's Chinatown, where she could call her parents in China for $3 a minute. It only took a few minutes for Yuan Yuan's mother to convince her to say yes to the San Francisco offer.

Yuan Yuan took Tomasson's offer and became the youngest solo dancer in the company. She rented an apartment in San Francisco and started taking English lessons. The lessons did not last long. She rehearsed all the time, so she ended up teaching herself English and learning from the other ballet dancers. They became her friends and were her family away from home.

Yuan Yuan learned quickly—both English and dance. It was a good thing, because Tomasson asked her at the last minute to fill in for a dancer who was injured. Yuan Yuan had to learn the new role in 24 hours. It was a complicated ballet by George Balanchine, set to Stravinsky's Violin Concerto. Yuan Yuan had never even seen the ballet, much less danced it. She watched the tape of the ballet over and over. A day later, she danced the part.

After Yuan Yuan was with the San Francisco Ballet for one year, Tomasson made her a principal dancer. She was just 19 and the youngest principal dancer in the company's history!

Yuan Yuan moved up the ranks into main roles, like prima ballerina—the main female dancer—faster than ballet dancers usually do.

Many people think that the San Francisco Ballet is the best ballet company in North America. Some even say it's the best in the world. Yuan Yuan's name draws crowds because they know that she is such an amazing dancer. She has been the prima ballerina in dozens of ballets, including *Swan Lake, Romeo and Juliet, The Nutcracker,* and *Othello*. Yuan Yuan has been with the San Francisco Ballet for more than 25 seasons—longer than any other principal dancer in the history of the company.

Yuan Yuan's dancing stands out among her peers. One of her first male dance partners in San Francisco was Colombian leading man Felipe Diaz. Felipe said that Yuan Yuan had an incredible stage presence from the beginning. Stage presence is the way some artists just shine onstage and you can't take your eyes off them. It's a **rare** gift. Octavio Roca, who reviews dance for the *San Francisco Chronicle*, said that Yuan Yuan showed "unsuspected fire." Tomasson still remembers Yuan Yuan's first dance in San Francisco, even after watching and directing dozens of dances and dancers over the years.

Other cities and countries have offered her roles, but Yuan Yuan said that she wants to stay in San Francisco. She was the first Chinese prima ballerina in the United States. She is a beloved figure in San Francisco. The mayor of San Francisco even proclaimed April 9, 2018, "Yuan Yuan Tan Day" in the city and county of San Francisco!

EXPLORE MORE! Yuan Yuan wrote a book called *Ballet and I* about her life's journey—growing up in a Shanghai alley to becoming a world-famous ballet artist.

DID YOU KNOW? Outside of dancing, Yuan Yuan does not do any exercise! When she's not rehearsing, her favorite thing to do is sleep. Her record is 15 straight hours. She's always ready to dance, though. She has no problem getting off a long plane ride and going straight to rehearsal. In 25 seasons, Yuan Yuan has only missed one major performance.

Alexandra
SCOTT
1996–2004

Alexandra Scott was a fighter and a champion for kids who have cancer, like herself. Her lemonade stand and the Alex's Lemonade Stand Foundation have raised millions of dollars for childhood cancer research. Although Alex died from cancer, she inspired many others to carry on her work.

Alexandra (Alex) Scott was born in Manchester, Connecticut, on January 18, 1996. She was the second of four kids born to parents Liz and Jay Scott. Just before she turned one, Alex's doctors found out that she had a **tumor** on her spine. It was a rare type of cancer.

The doctors told Alex's parents that, even if she lived, she would probably never walk. But, two weeks later, Alex's parents asked her to kick, and she moved her leg! That was the first sign of how Alex would live her life—bravely and with big, bold dreams.

Alex spent a lot of time in the hospital, where doctors and nurses tried to save her. She had to undergo many treatments. She went through **chemotherapy**, surgery, and **radiation**. She had surgery on her first birthday. The doctors spent several hours operating, but something went wrong. Alex was now paralyzed from the chest down. That meant she could no longer move her legs.

Still, Alex was determined to walk. Even though she was in pain and she stumbled, Alex wanted to blaze her own path. By the time she turned two, Alex was able to crawl. She could also stand up with the help of leg braces. Alex worked really hard and got stronger. She even learned how to walk without braces, just holding onto a walker! It seemed like she might beat the odds. But soon the doctors told her family that her **tumors** were back, and they were growing.

Then, Alex's parents found out about a doctor who was trying a new treatment for spinal cancer. They drove 11 hours from Connecticut to Philadelphia, despite Alex being in a lot of pain. After three days of radiation, Alex left Children's Hospital of Philadelphia much stronger and healthier.

But that did not last long, and the doctors proposed another procedure. On January 19, 2000, Alex got a **stem cell transplant**. The doctors removed Alex's cancer cells and replaced them with healthy cells from someone else.

Afterward, Alex told her mom, "I want to have a lemonade stand." At first, she sold lemonade once a month. Then, it was once a week. Soon, four-year-old Alex was setting up and selling lemonade every day. Her mom asked, "What is it that you want? I can just buy it for you."

Alex replied, "I'm not keeping the money. I'm giving it back to the hospital." Alex was raising money so her doctors could help other kids like her. With Alex's brother pitching in, her lemonade stand raised $2,000!

> **"IT'S SIMPLE, YOU SEE, FOR THIS WHOLE THING IS NOT ABOUT ME. AS LONG AS KIDS ARE SICK, I'LL DO WHAT I CAN. I'LL HELP RAISE MONEY THROUGH MY LEMONADE STAND."**

Alex made "lemonade out of lemons," or the best out of a bad situation. Her determination got people's attention. TV shows and magazines talked about how inspiring she was. Alex told one reporter that she wanted to raise a million dollars for kids with cancer. Her mom was shocked. Alex said that if every kid had a lemonade stand and donated, they could raise a million dollars.

People all over the world heard about the kid with cancer who was helping other children. They started to make their own lemonade stands and donate the proceeds. Within four years, kids ran 200 lemonade stands across the United States. Those children raised $200,000 for kids with cancer. That's when Alex's Lemonade Stand Foundation (ALSF) was born!

Alex's family moved to Philadelphia to be closer to her new doctors. It was winter, but Alex put on a hat and mittens and set up her lemonade stand. She loved selling lemonade, but not everything was great. Alex's best friend, Teresa, had cancer, too. Sadly, Teresa died. Alex was very sad and scared, but she did not let that stop her. She said, "I'm gonna do this lemonade stand in memory of Teresa."

The Philadelphia Inquirer, a local newspaper, wrote an article about Alex's Lemonade Stand. It showed a picture of Alex and mentioned her home address. People saw Alex in the news and lined up down the street and around the block to buy lemonade, cookies, and pizza. Many people paid more than the 50 cents that the glass of lemonade cost. Alex raised $12,000 that day!

Alex was getting famous. Superstar talk show host Oprah Winfrey invited her on TV to talk about her goal. Alex told Oprah that the most anyone ever paid for a glass of lemonade was $500. Then, Oprah presented Alex with a check from the Kellogg's cereal company for $25,000! After the *Oprah* show, Alex went to New York to appear on *The Today Show*. Though she was in pain, she didn't cancel the interview. Alex raised $1,000 in two minutes.

As Alex was getting weaker, kids across the country kept raising money. Finally, with one big donation from the car company Volvo, Alex reached her goal, raising $1 million for cancer research! Alex kept up her fight for as long as she could. But when she was eight, the cancer spread and got worse, and she died.

Today, Alex's family keeps her dream alive through the Alex's Lemonade Stand Foundation. Kids all over the world set up lemonade stands and raise money in her honor. Alex achieved more in her eight short years than many people do in 80 years. Her first goal was to raise one million dollars. People said that was impossible for a child. But Alex sparked a movement that raised eighty times that amount! Her foundation has now raised more than $80 million for childhood cancer research.

Alex's example and her story are remarkable. Her story is not just about money, but also about individual children. Alex's mom once heard about a boy struggling with the same kind of cancer Alex had. He was taking a medicine that Alex helped bring into **clinical trials**. Because of Alex, her mom said, "He ... is a kid now who is enjoying life and has a baseball game this weekend." Alex gave back and saved many other kids' lives. That is the mark of a true hero.

EXPLORE MORE! Read *Alex and the Amazing Lemonade Stand* by Alex's parents, Jay and Liz Scott.

DID YOU KNOW? A racehorse named Afleet Alex helps raise money for Alex's Lemonade Stand Foundation. Every time the horse wins a race, some of the winnings are donated to help fund cancer research. Whenever the horse competes, the owners encourage the racetracks to set up lemonade stands to raise funds.

Malala
YOUSAFZAI
1997–present

Malala Yousafzai is the youngest person to ever win a Nobel Peace Prize—the highest award in the world given to someone who works for peace. When girls weren't allowed to go to school anymore in Pakistan, Malala spoke out against that unfair law. She was shot for speaking out. Malala survived and continues to work to make sure that girls everywhere can get an education.

Malala Yousafzai was born on July 12, 1997, in Pakistan's Swat Valley. Girls were not as valued as boys in Pakistan, but her parents were very happy to have a baby girl. Malala's father, Ziauddin, wanted to make sure his daughter grew up with the same opportunities any boy would have—and that included getting an education.

Malala's father was a teacher who ran a school where girls and boys learned alongside each other. In 2008, that changed. A violent religious and political group called the Taliban took over Malala's hometown. They made a bunch of new rules aimed against girls and women.

The Taliban decided that girls could not go to school anymore. They weren't allowed to speak to men, except those who were close relatives like their brother or father. After a huge earthquake struck Pakistan, the Taliban said that it was punishment for women having too much freedom. They destroyed schools and made things like computers, books, and TVs illegal to own.

Malala's father hid their TV in a closet. Malala hid books in her shawl. The Taliban got stronger in Pakistan, but Malala's father spoke out against them. Malala was inspired by her father's activism. In 2008, 11-year-old Malala gave her first big speech: *How dare the Taliban take away my basic right to education?* It was even on TV in Pakistan. Speaking out against the Taliban was brave but very dangerous.

Shortly after, Malala wrote a blog for the British Broadcasting Corporation (BBC) about what life was like living under Taliban rule. She used the name Gul Makai, so the Taliban wouldn't know who she really was. But, after a while, they figured out that it was Malala writing posts against them.

The Taliban finally let girls under the age of 10 go back to school. Malala pretended she was younger than her real age, 11, and went to a secret school taught by Madam Maryam. It made Malala very angry that she had to sneak around to read and learn. Then, things got much worse.

The Taliban army took over Mingora, where Malala's family was living, and made everyone leave. Malala, her brothers, and her mother walked 15 miles and stayed with relatives in another town. She spent six weeks apart from her father, who was in Peshawar, Pakistan's capital, looking for support against the Taliban's restrictive rules. When Malala and her father were together again, they had an important meeting with an American politician living in Pakistan named Richard Holbrooke. They hoped he could help them fight for girls' education.

The world was beginning to notice that Malala was making an impact. In 2011, the Pakistan government gave her the country's first National Peace Prize for Youth. Today, it is called the National Malala Peace Prize. Malala was getting a lot of attention, but it was not all positive. The Taliban issued death threats in newspapers and even slipped threatening notes under her door. Her parents urged 15-year-old Malala to stop being so outspoken and focus on her studies. But she would not quit.

In October 2012, Malala was riding the bus home from school when Taliban soldiers with guns boarded her school bus. "Which one of you is Malala?" they shouted. When the kids all looked at Malala, a soldier shot her in the head. Ten days later, she woke up in a hospital in England—5,000 miles away from Pakistan.

Malala couldn't speak, but she could write. She asked what happened to her and if her father had also been shot. People from all over the world sent Malala cards, toys, and flowers. Famous people, like movie stars and singers, wrote to Malala wishing her a speedy recovery.

The United Nations, a group of more than 100 countries working for peace, declared that November 10 would be Malala Day to show the world's support for her.

Malala was lucky to be alive, but she had a long way to go to a full recovery. Because her brain had been injured in the shooting, Malala had to learn how to walk and talk all over again. Her family stayed in England because going back to Pakistan was far too dangerous. The Taliban still wanted to silence Malala.

In England, girls can do anything boys can do, including going to school. Women also hold the same jobs as men. By April of 2013, Malala felt well enough to start school again. In July, she was invited to speak at the United Nations in New York. It was her 16th birthday. In her speech, Malala asked the world leaders to make sure all children, including girls, could go to school. Everyone stood up and clapped after she finished speaking.

"ONE BOOK, ONE PEN, ONE CHILD, AND ONE TEACHER CAN CHANGE THE WORLD."

When she was 17, Malala won the Nobel Peace Prize. She was the youngest person ever to win the award. Part of the prize was a large amount of money. Malala used the money to open an all-girls school. She also started a foundation to fight for girls' rights.

Malala's voice wasn't silenced by the Taliban. Instead, her struggle made her stronger. She started studying at Oxford University when she was 20 years old. She loved the university and her new friends, but she missed Pakistan. Finally, five years after the Taliban attacked her, it was safe for Malala to return to Mingora.

Hundreds of friends and family members gathered around to celebrate Malala's homecoming. She was so happy! Malala graduated from Oxford in 2020. Since then, she has written books, given speeches on big stages and TV shows, and continued her work as an activist for girls' education.

Malala inspired millions of girls and women to stand up and speak out for their right to attend school. The United Nations even started the Malala petition to make sure that all children can go to school. More than three million people signed it. In 2012, the Pakistani government reacted to the petition and made a new law granting free education to every girl and boy between the ages of 5 and 16.

EXPLORE MORE! You can read about Malala's story from Malala herself in her autobiography, *I Am Malala.*

DID YOU KNOW? Malala decided to forgive the man who shot her. She believes that world peace begins with each person being at peace themselves. She would rather put her energy into fighting for the rights of the more than 130 million girls who still aren't able to go to school than stay mad at her attacker.

Simone
BILES
1997–present

When she was just 19 years old, Simone Biles became the most decorated American gymnast. During her career, Simone has won seven Olympic medals and 25 World Championship medals—19 of them gold. She won four gold medals at the 2016 Olympics—the first female gymnast from the United States to do so.

Simone Biles was born in Columbus, Ohio, on March 14, 1997. She was the youngest of four siblings. When Simone's father left the family, their mother, Shanon, was not able to take care of her children. They were all placed in foster care when Simone was only three years old.

The Biles children lived with a foster family for a short time. When Ronald, Simone's grandfather, found out that his grandchildren were in foster care, he came to get them. One of Simone's sisters and her brother were adopted by their Aunt Harriet. Simone and her other sister, Adria, were adopted by Ronald and his wife, Nellie. They lived happily together in Spring, Texas. Both girls called their grandparents Mom and Dad.

Simone's family had a trampoline in the backyard. She bounced and flipped for hours! When she was six, Simone went on a field trip to a gymnastics center. She loved it there. She was enchanted by the girls doing backflips and cartwheels on the floor and balance beam. Simone wanted to do everything they did.

Simone's grandparents signed her and Adria up for gymnastics classes. Simone came alive at the gym! She was a natural gymnast who quickly advanced to more difficult exercises. By the time she turned eight, she practiced on the balance beam, uneven bars, vault, and floor exercise. The floor was her favorite event. Simone's coach, Aimee Boorman, helped her train for hours every day after school. When she was just 11 years old, Simone joined junior elite—an advanced program for younger gymnasts. She started winning competitions against older gymnasts.

In 2011, Simone went to the USA Gymnastics National Championships to try to win a spot on the national team, but she didn't make the cut. Instead of quitting, Simone decided to work harder, which meant practicing even more.

The hard work paid off. At 14, Simone started her elite career when she competed in the 2011 American Classic in Houston. She came in third in the all-around and first on vault and balance beam. In 2012, Simone made the Junior National Team. At that point, Simone decided to be homeschooled so she could train at the gym for up to eight hours every day.

When the 2012 Olympics were on TV, Simone watched and cheered for the American gymnasts. She dreamed of going to the Olympics, too. When she turned 16, Simone became a senior elite gymnast and started competing against girls she had admired for years, like Gabby Douglas, Aly Raisman, and Kyla Ross. She was on her way to becoming a gymnastics star!

Simone was not always confident in herself. One time, she was so shaky with nerves on the beam that she fell off and hurt her ankle. She was worried that the injury would end her career. Instead of quitting, she trained harder to compete. Simone worked with a sports psychologist—a doctor who listened to her talk about her fears. She admitted that she felt pressure to win and didn't want to let her family and friends down. The doctor told Simone to just do her best and have fun. That's exactly what Simone did!

With her new attitude, Simone competed in the 2013 World Gymnastics Championships in Belgium. Always looking for something more difficult, Simone amazed the crowd with a difficult new move on the vault. It was a roundoff into a back handspring onto the vault with a half-turn and a two-twists landing. That move became known as "the Biles." Simone ended the competition as the all-around national champion! She was the first Black athlete to earn that title, and, finally, Simone was enjoying herself again. Over the next two years, Simone set another record by winning the most world championships of any gymnast ever!

When it was time for Simone to go to college, she had a decision to make. She got into the University of California, Los Angeles (UCLA) but decided not to go right away, so she could become a professional gymnast. She would not have been allowed to compete in college gymnastics while working toward that goal. Professional gymnasts make money when they win and also get paid to wear or advertise products.

Instead, Simone put her energy into making the 2016 Olympic team. After she competed in the Olympic trials in San Jose, California, Simone's dream came true. She made the team! Aly Raisman, Gabby Douglas, Laurie Hernandez, and Madison Kocian were her teammates. The girls called themselves the Final Five because 2016 was the last time there would be five, not four, gymnasts competing in the Olympics.

> **"I DON'T THINK ABOUT SIZE—I FOCUS MORE ON BEING POWERFUL AND CONFIDENT. I FEEL LIKE I'M SMALL AND MIGHTY AND PACK A POWERFUL PUNCH."**

Despite all their successes, Simone and many other women gymnasts were facing a terrible time. They were abused by a sports doctor for USA Gymnastics. When stories came to light about the doctor's illegal actions, Simone, Aly, and other girls stepped forward to speak out against him. Thanks to the bravery of Simone and girls like her, the doctor was eventually charged in court and put in prison.

In July 2016, Simone and the other girls flew to Rio de Janeiro, Brazil, for the 2016 Olympics. Simone and her teammates competed against each other, but they also competed as a team against other countries. The Final Five won the gold medal for the US team. When it was time for the individual competition, Simone was on fire! She won a gold medal for the all-around competition and vault. Then, she earned a bronze medal on the beam. For her final floor routine, Simone got an almost perfect score and won a fourth Olympic gold medal, making her the first US female gymnast to win that many medals at the Olympics.

Simone was chosen to carry the flag for Team USA in the closing ceremony. That wasn't the end of her story—or medal count. At the 2018 World Championships, Simone won four gold medals, making her career total 20 medals—more than any female gymnast ever. In 2021, she became the first woman in history to win seven all-around titles, upping her total to 21 medals.

In the weeks leading up to the 2020 Olympics, Simone started struggling with her mental health. In Tokyo, Simone developed the "twisties." This is when a gymnast's brain and body movements are not in sync. They can't tell up from down while they are in the air spinning, and that can be very dangerous. Simone knew she could have been injured, so she decided to center herself and skip a few events. She was determined to put her mental health first.

Simone said, "We also have to focus on ourselves because, at the end of the day, we're human, too. We have to protect our mind and our body, rather than just go out there and do what the world wants us to do." Today, many people consider Simone Biles to be the greatest gymnast in the world.

EXPLORE MORE! Feeling inspired and want to learn more about women like Simone? Check out *Bold Women in History: 15 Women's Rights Activists You Should Know* by Meghan Vestal.

DID YOU KNOW? After winning so many championships and medals, Simone wanted to help other kids learn how to do gymnastics. She worked to raise money for the Special Olympics, a sports competition for athletes who have disabilities. Simone thought about retiring to volunteer at events like that, but she decided to train for the 2020 Tokyo Olympics.

Amanda
GORMAN
1998–present

Amanda Gorman is a poet and activist. She was invited to read her poetry at the White House for former President Barack Obama. In 2021, Amanda became the youngest person ever to deliver a poem at a presidential **inauguration**, that of President Joe Biden. Her poem, "The Hill We Climb," made her famous and became a bestselling book.

On March 7, 1998, Amanda and her twin sister, Gabrielle, were born in Los Angeles, California. The girls were born several weeks early. They have an older brother named Spencer. Their mom, Joan Wicks, was a sixth-grade English teacher. She raised Amanda and her siblings on her own.

Amanda was not allowed to watch much TV as a kid. She could only watch shows from the 1940s. If she wanted to see something else, she had to write and give a speech to her mom saying why! Instead, her mother encouraged her to read and write. But, because Amanda was born early, she got many ear infections as a child.

The infections caused a hearing difficulty that made it hard for her to hear certain sounds when people spoke. So, she had trouble pronouncing some sounds, including the letter *r*. Amanda had something called a **speech impediment**, and she went to speech therapy at school.

At five years old, Amanda started writing songs. She realized that she didn't have a lot of musical talent, though, so she began writing poetry. When she got older, Amanda was invited to the United Nations. There, she heard Malala Yousafzai (page 25) give an inspirational speech. So, at 15, Amanda applied to be a youth delegate for the United Nations. She was chosen to give her opinion on issues that matter to young people in the United States.

Amanda read her poetry in competitions, and when she was 16, she was chosen as the first Los Angeles Youth **Poet Laureate**! Her poetry was so moving that city officials wanted her to read it to people all over town. Amanda represented the city as its best young poet.

Amanda attended New Roads School, a private high school. After classes and on weekends she worked at WriteGirl, a **nonprofit** organization helping teen girls find their voices through writing. Then, at just 17 years old, Amanda published her first book, *The One for Whom Food Is Not Enough*. After graduating from high school, Amanda got a scholarship to one of the best colleges in the country, Harvard University! That same year, she founded a nonprofit organization called One Pen One Page. It helps youth improve their writing and leadership skills.

While Amanda was studying at Harvard, she continued to write poetry and began to be recognized for it. Amanda became the first National Youth Poet Laureate in April 2017, when she was 19 and in her second year of college. As the National Youth Poet Laureate, Amanda traveled around the United States and started getting a lot of attention for her poems and the graceful way in which she delivered them. Her efforts raised awareness and appreciation of poetry writing and reading.

That same year, Amanda became the first youth poet to recite a poem at the opening of the Library of Congress's **literary** season. Amanda recited her poem "In This Place (An American Lyric)." It was at this reading that Amanda met Dr. Jill Biden, the wife of future president Joe Biden.

Amanda is an innovator as well as a poet. She won a grant from an organization called OZY that gives out $10,000 awards every year to college students who have amazing ideas. Amanda won a grant for her idea called Generation Empathy. Through a technology called virtual reality, people could learn to be kinder and more compassionate. Using a device like goggles or a computer, people could experience the world as if they were walking in someone else's shoes.

When Joe Biden was elected president of the United States, his wife, Jill, remembered how moved she was by Amanda's poetry. So, Amanda was asked to read a poem at the 2021 Presidential Inauguration. Amanda spent a lot of time researching, writing, and rehearsing her new poem, "The Hill We Climb." She spoke of hope, healing, coming together, and being strong. Amanda told reporter Anderson Cooper, "For most of my life, until two or maybe three years ago, I couldn't say the letter *r*. Even to this day sometimes I struggle with it." But Amanda did not let that stop her. She practiced a lot to get the *r*'s just right!

> **"FOR THERE IS ALWAYS LIGHT,
> IF ONLY WE'RE BRAVE ENOUGH
> TO SEE IT. IF ONLY WE'RE
> BRAVE ENOUGH TO BE IT."**

Right after the inauguration, the whole world wanted to know who Amanda Gorman was. She appeared on the February cover of *Time* magazine. They called her a "phenom," which means that she is a big, up-and-coming deal and someone to watch. The popular fashion magazine *Vogue* put her on its cover—she was the first poet ever to appear there! Even the National Football League wanted her to present. Amanda became the first poet to deliver a poem before the Super Bowl.

Through it all, Amanda continued to practice her speaking skills. She said that she uses songs as speech therapy. Her favorite song to practice speaking is the song from the musical *Hamilton* called "Aaron Burr, Sir." Amanda said, "It is jam-packed with *r*'s. If I can keep up with the actor in this track, then I am on my way to being able to say this *r* in a poem."

After Amanda appeared at President Biden's inauguration, her poem was published and became a bestselling book. Then, she published a children's book called *Change Sings: A Children's Anthem* and a collection of poems titled *Call Us What We Carry: Poems*. Amanda also became the youngest board member of 826 National, a nonprofit writing organization for kids. Amanda has stated that she plans to run for president in 2036!

Amanda's poems are often about the African **diaspora**, women's rights, and equal rights for all people. Her words and the way she says them speak to millions of people. Black girls see a role model and believe that they, too, could become a famous poet. And kids with speech impediments sit in awe that Amanda did not let her trouble saying *r*'s stop her!

EXPLORE MORE! Read Amanda Gorman's *The Hill We Climb*, a book made from the poem she read at President Biden's inauguration, or *Change Sings*, her picture book.

DID YOU KNOW? Amanda has been asked to perform by President Obama at the White House; by President Biden at his inauguration; by famous poet, playwright, and *Hamilton* creator Lin-Manuel Miranda; by human rights activist Malala Yousafzai, her original inspiration to join the UN Youth Delegate Program; and by many others.

Yusra
MARDINI
1998–present

Yusra Mardini is a Syrian **refugee** and swimmer. When she was 17 years old, she saved other refugees from drowning as they escaped by boat. Yusra went on to compete in the 2016 Olympics in Rio de Janeiro, Brazil, swimming with the first-ever Refugee Olympic Team.

Yusra Mardini was born in Darayya, Syria, on March 5, 1998. Her father was a swimming coach and he made sure that both Yusra and her older sister, Sara, learned to swim before they could even walk. Both girls dreamed of being in the Olympics as they watched swimmer Michael Phelps on TV. Yusra started swimming with the Syrian Olympic Committee, but then Syria erupted into civil war.

Both Mardini girls continued swim practice despite the war, until things took a serious turn. One day, an unexploded, rocket-propelled grenade came crashing through the roof and landed in the swimming pool where Yusra was training. In a different attack, Yusra's house was destroyed. In August 2015, she and her sister decided to leave Syria.

Yusra and Sara made their way through Lebanon, and then Turkey. Next, they got on a boat and paid to be smuggled to Greece. The inflatable rubber boat was only meant to carry six or seven people, but 20 refugees packed themselves inside it. On the way across the Aegean Sea, the boat's motor stopped working and the boat began to sink.

Most of the people on board didn't know how to swim. Yusra, Sara, and two other people who could also swim jumped into the water. For three and a half hours, they swam while holding onto the boat. They pulled the boat and kept it from sinking, saving the lives of the 16 other people. Finally, they got to Lesbos, Greece. To this day, Yusra still doesn't like swimming in the open sea.

From there, the sisters traveled through Europe and finally ended up in Berlin, Germany. The trip took them 25 days. As hard as the journey was, they always had each other. Along the way, they met and walked with 30 other refugees from Pakistan, Afghanistan, and other Middle Eastern countries. Yusra learned that it is important to help other people without ever asking for anything in return. Refugees from all different countries came together. It didn't matter what color their skin was or where they were from. They all just said, "We are refugees. We are headed to Germany and we are going to stick together."

When Yusra and Sara first arrived in Germany, they did not like their new surroundings at all. They were living in an overcrowded refugee camp. But, Yusra was very grateful to Germany for opening their doors to Syrian refugees so she could make a new life and keep swimming!

Once she settled into her new home, Yusra began training for the Olympics with her coach, Sven Spannekrebs. Yusra was hoping to become good enough to compete in the 200-metre freestyle swimming event. Finally, she was picked to be one of 10 Refugee Olympic Team members who represented over 65 million people forced to leave their countries. Just a year before, swimming had saved her life while escaping war. Now she would swim in the 2016 Summer Olympics in Rio de Janeiro, Brazil!

At the Olympics, Yusra swam in the 100-metre butterfly and the 100-metre freestyle events. While she didn't win a medal, Yusra won the butterfly against four other swimmers in one of the competitions. Her time was 1:09.21—just over a minute—to swim from one end of the pool to the other. After she swam, Yusra was very happy. She said, "Everything was amazing. The only thing I ever wanted was to compete in the Olympics."

After the Olympics, Yusra started giving important speeches about refugees. The media took notice. Yusra earned many awards, including being named in 2016 one of *Time* magazine's 30 Most Influential Teens—teenagers who influence, or inspire others to change by example. That same year, *People* magazine put her on their list of 25 Women Changing the World. Since then, Yusra has addressed the United Nations General Assembly and met world leaders, including US President Barack Obama and Pope Francis.

Sports gave Yusra a strong voice. She uses that voice to help refugees find safer places to live by acting as a **goodwill ambassador** for the United Nations. As an ambassador, Yusra tries to change how people view refugees. Her story is one of hope, courage, and determination. Yusra showed the world that people who flee their countries can go on to do great things.

> **"I WANT TO REPRESENT ALL THE REFUGEES. I WANT TO SHOW EVERYONE THAT, AFTER THE PAIN, AFTER THE STORM, COMES CALM DAYS."**

"The war was hard," Yusra says. "Sometimes we couldn't train because of the war. Or sometimes you had training, but there was a bomb in the swimming pool." Yusra learned that many refugees suffer even after they leave their country. "It's tough. It was really hard for everyone, and I don't blame anyone if they cried. But, sometimes you just have to move on. . . . In the water, there is no difference if you are a refugee, or a Syrian, or German."

In Germany, her new coach saw how serious Yusra was and asked if she just liked swimming or really wanted to achieve something. She told him that she wanted to go back to the Olympics. She succeeded and competed in the 100-metre butterfly at the 2020 Olympic Games in Tokyo.

Since competing in Rio in 2016, Yusra has been a voice for refugees and shown others that life can go on after being displaced, or forced to leave your home country. She helps leaders of countries understand that they should open borders for refugees. Yusra didn't always like being described as a refugee. But now, she uses that word as a badge of honor and has become the face of refugees everywhere.

EXPLORE MORE! Yusra wrote an autobiography about her Olympic journey called *Butterfly: From Refugee to Olympian—My Story of Rescue, Hope, and Triumph.*

DID YOU KNOW? At the 2016 Rio Olympic Games, Yusra was afraid of how people would react to the first-ever Refugee Olympic Team. But then, she and nine other athletes—from South Sudan, Congo, Ethiopia, and Syria—walked out behind a flag bearing the colorful Olympic rings with the crowd cheering loudly. Refugees wrote to Yusra telling her how she inspired them. She never wanted to be a hero—all she ever wanted to do was swim.

Ashima
SHIRAISHI
2001-present

Rock climber Ashima Shiraishi became the top female rock climber in the world when she was just 15 years old. She started climbing when she was only six. By the time she was 10, she was climbing boulders that few grown women have successfully climbed.

Ashima Shiraishi was born in New York City on April 3, 2001. Her parents were Japanese **immigrants** who came to the United States in 1978. Her father, Hisatoshi "Poppo" Shiraishi, was a traditional Japanese dancer. After Ashima was born, Poppo noticed that his daughter seemed to never stop moving her arms and legs. When Ashima was six, Poppo took her to Central Park to climb 30-foot-tall Rat Rock, which is very popular with boulderers.

In 2008, when she was seven, Ashima began to compete in rock climbing. For the first four years, she was coached by Obe Carrion, who was very skilled at the sport. But Ashima's father and Obe did not agree on how to work with Ashima, so Poppo started coaching his daughter when she was 11 years old.

It seems like Ashima was born to climb. She has little but strong fingers to grip the rocks, a small body (she is five foot one and weighs less than 90 pounds), and a knack for finding the best way up a boulder. She can find small grooves in the rock, called holds, where she can fit her fingers or toes in places most people would not be able to see. Climbing rocks is not like climbing a ladder. A climber needs to pull themselves up by twisting and turning their body into different positions. Ashima looks like a graceful praying mantis when she climbs.

When Ashima climbs boulders, the rocks are usually no more than 20 feet high. Climbers call each boulder a "problem," like a math problem, because they have to figure out how to get to the top. The boulder climbers don't wear a harness and are not usually attached to ropes. If they fall, they will be in major pain. Ashima and other people who climb use gymnastics chalk to keep their hands dry so they can hold on to the rocks with their fingertips without slipping.

Each boulder climb is rated on something called a V Scale: V0 is the easy end and V17 is the most difficult. When she was eight, Ashima climbed a boulder called the *Power of Silence* in Hueco Tanks, Texas. It is ranked a V10. When she was nine, she conquered *Chablanke* (a V11/12) and *Roger in the Shower* (a V11), as well as several other Texas boulders that were very tough to climb. At age 10, Ashima climbed the *Crown of Aragorn* (V13) and became the youngest person ever to climb a V13—and one of just a few women to successfully complete the climb.

Ashima is great at climbing boulders, but she is also very skilled at lead climbing. For this technique, she finds metal bolts already in the rocks and attaches ropes to them as she climbs. In October 2012, when she was just 11, Ashima climbed 90-foot-tall *Southern Smoke* at the Red River Gorge. She was the youngest person to lead climb such a difficult route.

Always looking for a bigger challenge, Ashima climbed her first V14, *Golden Shadow*, in July 2014. She was the second female climber, after Tomoko Ogawa, to make it to the top of a V14—and she was only 13 years old! *Golden Shadow* was just a warm-up. On January 1, 2015, 14-year-old Ashima climbed her second V13/14, *The Swarm*, and became the first female to reach the top.

"CLIMB THROUGH YOUR PROBLEMS. FAILURE IS A HUGE PART OF SUCCESS."

Sometimes people compare Ashima to great athletes from other sports. For example, the *New Yorker* called her a "Gretzky of granite," since hockey player Wayne Gretzky was so talented on ice. Others compare her to tennis great Roger Federer or ballet talent Misty Copeland. The *New Yorker* also called her "the wall dancer" because she makes climbing rocks look graceful.

In 2016, Ashima traveled to her parents' homeland of Japan. She had her eyes set on the *Horizon*—a V15 boulder on Mount Hiei. Ashima completed the climb and became the first woman to ever climb a V15. She was also the youngest climber to complete it. At the time, V16 boulders were the most difficult climbs anyone in the world had been able to complete. Since then, Ashima climbed *Horizon* a second time and completed a new V15: *Sleepy Rave* in Australia.

Today, Ashima has several awards under her belt. She won gold medals in 2015, 2016, and 2017 for both lead climbing and bouldering in the IFCS Climbing World Championships. At one of the world championships, Ashima was the only climber, out of any age group, to reach the top of all four boulders—three out of four on her first try! In 2017, she came in second in the women's Bouldering Nationals. Her competition was Alex Puccio, who had won the event nine times before.

National Geographic recognized Ashima's amazing achievements and named her one of its Adventurers of the Year in 2017. Ashima was finally able to compete as an adult in the 2019 Bouldering Nationals for Women and took home the gold medal!

Throughout her life, Ashima has shown determination and focus as she continues to push her limits in climbing. She hoped to compete in the 2020 Olympics in Japan. It was the first time climbing was included in the games. Unfortunately, she didn't make the four-person team.

Competition was fierce and there were only two spots for women.

To be sure, Ashima will continue her ascent to be one of the world's most talented and experienced climbers. She says, "I am Ashima. What I do is climb. What I do is solve problems, which is to say, I make them mine."

EXPLORE MORE! Ashima wrote a children's book called *How to Solve a Problem: The Rise (and Falls) of a Rock-Climbing Champion.*

DID YOU KNOW? Ashima's father is a butoh artist, a Japanese dancer. He was a famous street performer in New York who was hard to miss, painted gold from head to toe and only wearing his underwear. Sometimes he danced with a dummy that was on fire. Other times, he rode on top of a taxi or stood for 20 minutes, barefoot, on top of a block of ice!

Autumn
DE FOREST
2001–present

Autumn de Forest is an American painter who is known as an artistic child prodigy. She started painting when she was five and hasn't stopped since. She sticks to a strict schedule to create her art and has sold over $7 million in paintings! Today Autumn teaches kids how to paint.

Born on October 27, 2001, Autumn de Forest lives with her parents in Las Vegas, Nevada. Her father, Douglas, is a musician, and her mother, Katherine, used to be a model and actress. Autumn is the descendant of several artists descendants on her father's side, including Lockwood de Forest, George de Forest, and Robert W. de Forest. Beginning in 1913, Robert was president of the board of trustees of the world-famous Metropolitan Museum of Art in New York City.

When Autumn was four, she painted a watercolor in preschool. She called it "Elephant." Her parents thought it looked very advanced for a preschooler. Then, when Autumn was five, her father was staining furniture in the garage. Autumn asked for something to paint, too. Douglas happily gave her a piece of wood and some stain. When he saw what she painted, he was surprised. He thought it looked like something famous painter Mark Rothko would paint—something far more artistic than a child at age five normally paints.

Seeing that their daughter clearly had an eye for painting, Autumn's parents bought her paints, canvases, and brushes. Many canvases were bigger than she was! They even turned their home music studio into an art studio for Autumn. She spent hours painting in the studio every day.

When she was seven, Autumn told her parents that she wanted to display her art for other people to see. In 2009, the family got a booth at the Boulder City Fine Arts Festival. Many people thought it was her father who made the paintings. Autumn got an honorable mention award at that art fair. Just a month after that, she won Best of Show at another art event.

> **"MY GOAL AS AN ARTIST IS TO CREATE ART THAT MAKES PEOPLE LOOK AT THE WORLD IN A DIFFERENT WAY."**

It was not long before Autumn's parents got an agent to sell her work. In February of 2010, Autumn put her art in an auction. Within just 16 minutes, the eight-year-old artist sold more than $100,000 in paintings! One of her paintings sold for more than $25,000. Soon after, the Discovery Health Channel featured Autumn on TV in a special show about child prodigies. The world was noticing Autumn. Disney even paid her to paint a series of Disney princesses!

Autumn had her first solo show in 2017 at the Monthaven Arts and Cultural Center in Hendersonville, Tennessee. It was called "Her White Room: The Art of Autumn de Forest." That same year, Autumn was named one of *Teen Vogue*'s 21 Under 21. By that time, her paintings were being compared to those created by Pablo Picasso, Georgia O'Keeffe, and Andy Warhol.

It's hard to describe Autumn's style, because her pieces all look different and are made using various mediums. Autumn uses acrylic paint, oil paint, and a type of melted wax called encaustic on canvas. She never got formal training as an artist. Autumn just takes everyday objects, animals, and people and paints them in the styles of some of her favorite artists.

When it comes to painting techniques, Autumn has some pretty unique ones! Sometimes she drags a rope covered in paint across her canvas. She also uses an air compressor to blow paint around the canvas, creating colorful streaks that move out in all different directions. Autumn even created a whole "drip" series of paintings. One painting has beach balls dripping out of the sky. Others feature dripping hearts and cowboy hats.

Autumn finds inspiration in her dreams and the world around her. She's painted some masterpieces based on TV commercials. She also made several pieces centered on crayons. Autumn says that we take crayons for granted because kids use them every day. When she recreated the painting *American Gothic* by Grant Wood, she put a crayon in the farmer's hand instead of a pitchfork. The result, called *American Graphic,* was a colorful new take on the famous painting.

In 19 short years, Autumn has been given many honors. When she was 14, she painted a piece for Pope Francis, the leader of the Catholic Church. She even went to Rome to give it to him in person. While she was there, the pope honored her with the International Giuseppe Sciacca Award for making the world a better place through her art. The painting is now hanging in the Vatican collection! Autumn was also the youngest artist ever to be appointed, by former First Lady Michelle Obama, to the President's Committee for the Arts and Humanities.

Today, Autumn is not only selling her paintings for up to $50,000 apiece, she is also giving back to the community. She created the Autumn de Forest Foundation to help other kids create and use art to empower themselves. She also works with kids from underserved communities from all over the country who might not have access to art classes. She teaches them how to make art and feel good about their own talents and creations.

The Foundation has also donated more than half a million dollars to help relief efforts after the Boston bombing, Hurricane Sandy, and the earthquakes in Haiti, as well as many other causes. Autumn donates many of her paintings to charity art auctions. She speaks across the country, in schools, at corporations, and at universities about the importance of the arts. Autumn loves painting, but most of all, she loves helping others.

EXPLORE MORE! Learn about all kinds of artists, including Pablo Picasso who inspired Autumn's work in *Famous Artists in History: An Art History Book for Kids* by Kelly Milner-Halls.

DID YOU KNOW? Some of Autumn's paintings have stories behind them. *Goodnight Moon* shows a black house with one lit window, some birds on a telephone wire, and a full moon in the sky. She says the lit window stands for a grandmother who died. The birds on the wire are the children and grandchildren who loved her.

Greta
THUNBERG
2003–present

Greta Thunberg is a Swedish environmental activist who is famous for her tireless quest to raise awareness of climate change. When she was 15, she started protesting at Parliament—Sweden's government—pleading with her country to get serious about making changes to reverse global warming. Since then, Greta has spoken around the world and convinced other leaders to take action against climate change.

Greta Tintin Eleonora Ernman Thunberg was born on January 3, 2003, in Stockholm, Sweden. Her father is an actor, and her mother was an opera singer. When Greta was eight, she learned about global warming, how the Earth's warming temperatures are damaging the environment, and the threat to the planet. It made her very depressed, so she stopped talking. Greta also stopped eating and lost 22 pounds in two months.

Doctors diagnosed Greta with several conditions. One of them is Asperger's syndrome, which is a type of **autism**. Greta views her diagnosis as a superpower, not a disorder.

Greta also has obsessive-compulsive disorder (OCD), which is a mental health disorder. In addition, she has selective mutism, meaning she is unable to speak in some social situations. When she does speak, Greta is very honest and straightforward. She tells the truth in a very clear way.

Greta started combating climate change right in her own home. She told her parents that they were taking her future away by allowing the Earth to get so polluted that it might be dangerous for her and future generations. For two years, she made her family lower their **carbon footprint** by becoming vegan, not flying on airplanes, and reusing products instead of throwing them away.

Giving up flying meant that Greta's mother also had to give up her career as an opera singer. Her mother didn't really give up flying to save the climate. She did it for Greta, because she saw how much it meant to her. Greta said that her parents' support and willingness to change their lifestyle gave her hope. She believed that she could actually make an even bigger difference.

In May 2018, 15-year-old Greta wrote an essay about climate change for a contest in a Swedish newspaper and she won! In the article she wrote, "I want to feel safe. How can I feel safe when I know we are in the greatest crisis in human history?" Three months later, she decided to start making her country's leaders aware of the danger of global warming.

Greta had seen students in Florida striking for gun-free, safe schools, so she decided to go on strike herself. Greta was very motivated because Sweden, and most of Europe, was experiencing a huge heat wave and deadly wildfires. It was 2018—the hottest summer in Europe on record in 262 years!

> "YOU HAVE STOLEN MY DREAMS AND MY CHILDHOOD WITH YOUR EMPTY WORDS. . . . PEOPLE ARE SUFFERING. PEOPLE ARE DYING. ENTIRE ECOSYSTEMS ARE COLLAPSING. WE ARE IN THE BEGINNING OF A MASS EXTINCTION, AND ALL YOU CAN TALK ABOUT IS MONEY AND FAIRY TALES OF ETERNAL ECONOMIC GROWTH. HOW DARE YOU!"

Greta decided to skip school on a Friday to protest outside of the main government building, Parliament. She held a sign that read, in Swedish: *Skolstrejk för klimatet,* which means "school strike for climate." She demanded that the Swedish government cut carbon emissions—the pollution that comes out of cars and factories—and follow the rules of the Paris Agreement, which describes how much carbon each country can make.

Greta protested outside Parliament all by herself for three Fridays but a few months later, kids from all over the world started small protests in their towns. Even though she skipped school every Friday, Greta made sure all her schoolwork was done. She was one of the top five students in her class.

The global kids' climate strike movement became known as Fridays for Future. After that, climate strikes started happening every Friday somewhere around the world. By 2019, 2,500 protests were happening in 272 cities and 163 countries, with more than four million students worldwide!

When the 2019 United Nations Climate Action Summit took place in New York, Greta knew she needed to attend so she could speak. Instead of taking an environmentally unsafe plane, she sailed to North America on a boat that used solar and wind power! The trip took more than two weeks. Greta gave her most famous speech at the summit. Talking to world leaders, she shouted, "How dare you?" Greta was very angry that leaders were daring to leave the world in such bad shape for children like her.

Almost overnight, Greta became famous. She was the vocal leader of a new movement, but a lot of people didn't like her message—or how outspoken she was at such a young age. Still, many people—especially politicians—were listening. Newspapers started calling the positive changes toward climate change "the Greta Thunberg effect."

The list of honors and awards Greta has received is long. She was named one of *Time* magazine's 100 Most Influential People and then, in 2019, *Time* named her Person of the Year. She was not yet 17—the youngest person to be honored with that title. She also made the list of *Forbes* magazine's World's 100 Most Powerful Women. Most amazingly, Greta was nominated for the Nobel Peace Prize, one of the highest honors in the world, for three years in a row (2019, 2020, and 2021).

Greta has given speeches around the globe and met many famous people. She spoke to then-President Barack Obama in person, met with members of the US House of Representatives, and even met the pope. Greta is known for being very straightforward. At the 2019 World Economic Forum, Greta said, "Our house is on fire." She was talking about the fact that our planet is warming up very quickly, which is dangerous for all life on Earth.

In addition to her passionate speeches, Greta uses social media to spread her message. People started following her and sharing her posts. Someone from a bank in Finland called Nordea shared one of Greta's posts to more than 200,000 followers. In under a week, international media wanted to hear what Greta had to say.

Greta started out urging leaders to deal with the climate crisis all by herself. Today, millions of other students have joined her movement from all around the world. She does not—and will not—back down when speaking in front of powerful politicians. Shortly before she turned 18, Greta said, "I'm going to continue to do everything I can to push in the right direction, no matter what the circumstances are."

EXPLORE MORE! Read about how Greta views her learning differences as a superpower in *The Greta Thunberg Story: Being Different Is a Superpower* by Michael Part.

DID YOU KNOW? In September 2019, Greta and a group of 15 other children from different nations filed a complaint with the United Nations Committee on the Rights of the Child. Their targets were five countries that were not on target to cut down on pollution: Argentina, Brazil, France, Germany, and Turkey.

Autumn
PELTIER
2004–present

A utumn Peltier is the chief water commissioner for the Anishinabek Nation in Ontario, Canada, her homeland. She travels all over the world speaking about native people's rights to clean drinking water. Autumn is an activist and advocate for First Nations, or **Indigenous**, communities.

Autumn Peltier was born on September 27, 2004, on Manitoulin Island in Canada. She is of Ojibway/Odawa heritage, and grew up on the Wiikwemkoong First Nation reserve. (A reserve is land that was set aside by a government for Indigenous people to live on.) Autumn went to St. Mother Teresa High School. She has two sisters, Naomi and Ciara. They live with their mother, Stephanie, in Ottawa, Canada. Autumn's reserve is next to one of this planet's biggest freshwater lakes, Lake Huron.

When Autumn was eight, she started going to water ceremonies on First Nation reserves with her mother. At a ceremony on the Serpent River First Nation reserve in Ontario, Autumn asked her mother to use the restroom.

When she went to wash her hands, she saw all sorts of signs saying "Boil Water. Do Not Drink." When water is toxic, you usually must boil it before using it to get rid of any dangerous bacteria. Autumn had to sanitize her hands after washing them with that toxic water. She asked her mother why their water was so polluted. Autumn's mother didn't know why, but she told Autumn that the community there had been warned to boil water for more than 20 years! Autumn couldn't believe it.

Autumn's great-aunt, Josephine Mandamin, was the chief water commissioner for the Anishinabek Nation. As the chief water protector, Josephine had to open people's eyes about, and fight against, water pollution. She was called "Grandmother Water Walker" because she walked around the Great Lakes, speaking to anyone who would listen. Josephine taught Autumn about the importance of respecting and protecting clean water. They would pray and sing for clean water in traditional ceremonies.

But praying for water wasn't enough for Autumn—she needed to speak out and tell world leaders that First Nations reserves were like developing, or poorer, countries, even though they were in Canada. She was inspired to become a water protector and activist.

Autumn started going to water ceremonies all over Ontario. Then, in 2015 when she was 11, Autumn went to the Children's Climate Conference in Sweden. She was among dozens of children from all around the globe who came together to discuss how to combat climate change.

> "I ADVOCATE FOR WATER BECAUSE
> WE ALL CAME FROM WATER AND
> WATER IS LITERALLY THE ONLY
> REASON WE ARE HERE TODAY AND
> LIVING ON THIS EARTH."

In 2016, Autumn brought even more attention to the issue of clean water. When she was just 12 years old, Autumn went to a big meeting of the Assembly of First Nations. She got the chance to meet Canada's Prime Minister, Justin Trudeau. She was supposed to hand him a gift and was told not to say anything to him. But Autumn knew that this was her chance to make a real difference. When he reached for the gift, Autumn pulled it back and said, "I am very unhappy with the choices you've made and the broken promises to my people."

Trudeau replied, "I understand that." Right then and there, Autumn started crying at the thought of all her people having to boil water and walk miles to get clean water. Prime Minister Trudeau promised her, "I will protect the water." Autumn later said that when she looks back on her life and all the work she's done, that was her proudest moment. Boldly telling the prime minister that he wasn't doing his job right, in front of so many people, got Autumn a lot of media attention as a youth activist.

At age 13, Autumn was invited to speak in New York at the United Nations for World Water Day in March 2018. Several months later, in August, she delivered her message as the keynote speaker for World Water Week in Stockholm, Sweden. In 2019, she was invited back again to the UN Global Landscapes Forum. Each time, Autumn gave a moving speech to world leaders.

Autumn was awarded a medal by the lieutenant governor in Ontario for her amazing work in water conservation. She was also honored as an Ontario Junior Citizen and won a Youth in Action award. For three years in a row, from 2017 to 2019, Autumn was nominated for the International Children's Peace Prize. In 2019, Autumn was also honored as a Science Defender by the Union of Concerned Scientists.

Sadly, in February 2019, Autumn's great-aunt Josephine passed away. Just a few months later, when Autumn was only 14, she was named the new chief water commissioner for the Anishinabek Nation.

Autumn was given the 2021 RevolutionHer Community Vision Award for Youth because she is active in her community as a leader. Because of her hard work, 88 communities across Canada now have access to clean drinking water. But the government has more work to do on First Nations reserves. In about 61 communities, the water is not safe to drink yet, and the residents still need to boil it. Autumn's and others' efforts must continue.

Autumn's elders taught her to believe that water is sacred and has a spirit. Her people believe that water is important because we could not live without it. People are mainly made up of water, and water covers most of the planet. Autumn says that "water is the lifeblood of

Mother Earth. . . . [It] is around us and sustains us all."
Autumn learned the teachings of her great-aunt and
mother, and she continues to advocate for First Nations
people to have clean drinking water.

EXPLORE MORE! Read *Sadiq and the Clean Water
Crew* by Siman Nuurali and Christos Skaltsas or *Fresh
Air, Clean Water: Our Right to a Healthy Environment* by
Megan Clendenan.

DID YOU KNOW? People might think that they will
have clean, fresh water forever, but water can run out
or become too polluted to drink. Canada, where Autumn
lives, has about 7 percent of the world's renewable
freshwater. The Great Lakes, which Canada shares with
the United States, have about 20 percent of the world's
freshwater supply. Still, many places, like Flint, Michigan,
have contaminated drinking water.

Marley
DIAS
2005–present

Marley Dias is an author and activist who started the #1000BlackGirlBooks campaign. She collects books that have Black girls as the main characters and donates them to schools around the world. Marley even has her own show called *Bookmarks: Celebrating Black Voices*, where she interviews famous Black people.

Born on January 4, 2005, Marley Dias was named after the famous Jamaican reggae singer Bob Marley. Her family comes from Jamaica and Cape Verde, but Marley was born in Philadelphia, Pennsylvania, and raised in West Orange, New Jersey.

While Marley was growing up, her mom and dad had a great home library for her. In it, she could find lots of diverse books, including books with Black girls as the main characters. But at school, she only found books about white boys and their dogs. There wasn't enough diversity in the books that kids were reading. Marley told her mom she wanted to read books at school in which she could see Black girls that looked like her. She also wanted to make sure that other Black girls could see themselves reflected in the books they read.

So, in November of 2015, when she was 11 years old, Marley started a book drive called #1000BlackGirlBooks. Marley's goal was to gather 1,000 books with Black girls as main characters and give them to Black girls at other schools. She wanted to do that by February 2016.

Marley blew that goal out of the water! In just a few months, Marley gathered 9,000 books about and for Black girls like her. By doing this, Marley brought a lot of attention to the fact that most children's books were about white kids. Marley's book drive went viral. Reporters, bloggers, and kids in schools around the world started to donate books. As of 2022, Marley has collected more than 13,000 books! She even donated some books to schools in Jamaica.

Marley and her #1000BlackGirlBooks campaign quickly got noticed. She was invited to appear on popular TV shows like *The View* and *The Today Show*. She went on *The Nightly Show with Larry Wilmore*. And she became a speaker for the nonprofit organization Girls Can Do, whose mission is to inspire and encourage young women to "have big dreams and pursue them."

Marley also teamed up with *Elle* magazine, which made her the editor-in-chief of her own digital publication, called *Marley Mag*. In her new role, she got to interview the famous Black ballerina Misty Copeland, award-winning Black filmmaker Ava DuVernay, and former Secretary of State Hillary Clinton.

In 2018, at age 13, Marley wrote and published her very own book, *Marley Dias Gets It Done: And So Can You!* It's about how kids can use their passions—the things they feel strongly about—to create change in the world. In the book, she describes how kids can be "upstanders" by not just standing by when other kids are getting bullied. She says that showing kindness and respect to everyone in our community—from postal workers to custodians to teachers—is very important.

At age 15, Marley was asked to host her own Netflix show, *Bookmarks: Celebrating Black Voices.* Marley is both the host and the executive producer, which means she gets to make a lot of important decisions. On the show, she talks about books that focus on justice, respect, and how to take action in your community. Marley has interviewed dozens of influential Black people, including rapper, writer, and actor Common; author and actress Lupita Nyong'o; comedian Tiffany Haddish; and author Jacqueline Woodson.

> **"GIRLS OF COLOR AND YOUNG WOMEN NEED TO BE SEEN, HEARD, AND VALUED. SCHOOLS CAN MAKE THIS HAPPEN BY INCLUDING OUR STORIES IN THE CURRICULUM."**

Marley has spoken at the White House alongside then-First Lady Michelle Obama and TV show host Oprah Winfrey. *Time* magazine named her one of the

25 Most Influential Teens of 2018. The National Education Association (NEA) named her Ambassador for Read Across America. She has even been featured in ads for Disney World Resorts and Walmart's Black History Month campaign. She is the youngest person ever to be named to *Forbes* magazine's 30 Under 30 list. Marley has earned numerous awards, including from the magazines *Ebony* and *The Smithsonian*.

Marley says one trailblazer inspired her the most. Augusta Baker was a Black librarian and storyteller who worked in the New York Public Library for more than 35 years. Her mission was to make sure that Black people were celebrated for their achievements, especially in the books that children read. Augusta's and Marley's missions are very similar: to include the narrative, or life story, of Black people in books. Even though Marley never met Augusta, she feels very connected to her through their common goal.

Today, Marley takes suggestions for books from teachers, parents, librarians, and kids. She makes videos and posts on social media to spread the word about reading. Her #1000BlackGirlBooks campaign continues to inspire kids to advocate for having books that reflect who they are. She has shown that one girl can truly make a difference.

Marley Dias is an activist and spokesperson for reading and diversity in books. She believes that girls must be strong, smart, and brave to make change in the world. When she saw that her school didn't have books with characters that looked like her, or other Black girls, she set the goal of collecting 1,000 books and donating them. Marley's determination led her to quickly surpass that goal!

EXPLORE MORE! Read Marley Dias's book, *Marley Dias Gets It Done: And So Can You!*

DID YOU KNOW? Marley is clear that she is pushing for Black girls' stories and for other people's stories. She wants kids' differences to act as "windows" and "mirrors." By "mirrors," Marley means that she wants Black girls—like her—to have books that reflect their lives and histories, like a mirror. By "windows," she means that she wants every child to be able to peek into, and learn about, different cultures.

b[c] && ("parameter" == b[c].us
}
function(b);
occurrences(a, ",", !1);
$("#mode_single").hasClass("mode_selected")
$("#fin").pa
nt().addClass("wobbl
$(".genhov
nimated2");
setTimeout
nt().removeClass(
$("#fin
s("animated2");
$(".gen
50);
("visible");

Samaira
MEHTA
2008–present

Samaira Mehta is an Indian American **coder** who, at eight years old, founded a company called CoderBunnyz. The company gets its name from a board game she created that helps kids learn how to code, or write computer programs. Samaira held more than 500 workshops on coding and taught more than 10,000 kids—all before she was 13 years old.

Samaira Mehta was born on March 8, 2008, in Santa Clara, California. Her father, Rakesh, is an **engineer** at Intel, a technology company. He started teaching his daughter how to code when she was only six years old. He got her interested by playing a little prank on her. He put a button on his computer screen that said "Press this if you're beautiful." When Samaira moved the mouse control over the button to click it, it disappeared. Shocked, she asked her dad, "How did you do that?" He explained that he did it by coding. Samaira was hooked!

Samaira and her younger brother, Aadit, loved playing board games, and she loved coding. She thought it would be a great idea to combine the two into something fun that could teach people from ages 4 to 104 how to code. With Aadit's help, Samaira designed a board game called CoderBunnyz. She picked the name CoderBunnyz because she loves coding, board games, and bunnies! It took them about a year and a half to finish the game. She was eight years old when they completed the game.

Samaira's game teaches kids how to code using concepts that many computer languages use. It makes difficult coding concepts simple and uses farm animals to make it fun. In the game, players move bunnies along the board to try to eat as many carrots as possible.

According to Samaira, while she was making Coder-Bunnyz, people would not take her seriously because she was only six or seven years old. They thought that, because she was so young, she could not do great things yet. When the game was released in 2017, it quickly became the number one board game on a popular online store. Samaira earns money for the games she sells. CoderBunnyz is in high demand. Students in more than 106 schools use the game as part of their STEM (Science, Technology, Engineering, and Math) curriculum.

CoderBunnyz is also the name of the business Samaira founded at about the same time she developed her game. She is the CEO, or chief executive officer. This means she makes the decisions for the business and is in charge of everyone else. Her family is all part of the business. Samaira's mom helps her market, or sell, her games. Her little brother tests out her new inventions. Her dad is on the board of her company and gives her advice. In the beginning, the family packed every game up in a box and mailed it out.

In a video Samaira made about "a day in the life" as a CEO, she talked about how she uses a planner to organize her time and tasks. After all, she is a student and runs a business. She has to answer questions for magazine interviews, make videos for her coding games, and, of course, write code! Samaira's days as a "She-EO" (what girl/women CEOs are sometimes called) are very busy. At 13 years old, she is already a big boss!

"LEARNING IS SO MUCH EASIER WHEN IT IS FUN."

CoderBunnyz is not Samaira's only game. When her dad told her how he helped design the **artificial intelligence (AI)** computer chips for self-driving cars and drones, it got Samaira thinking. It's not easy to learn to use AI concepts online, so she decided to create CoderMindz, the world's first board game teaching kids (and adults) the skills they'd need to work in the field of AI. Kids have to train their robot using code cards to win. It uses concepts from the Java programming language. Not only did Samaira make the drawings for the game, she found a factory that would make the game. In 2020, she developed CoderMarz which combines her love of space and Mars with her interest in artificial intelligence.

One of Samaira's goals is to help one billion kids—especially girls—get access to what they need to learn coding. To do this, she started Yes, One Billion Kids Can Code. The program holds workshops and creates coding curriculums and apps. Samaira also wants to encourage kids to start their own businesses and become **entrepreneurs**, so she created a program called Boss Biz. It helps kids learn how to become the boss of their own business, like Samaira did. But she's not stopping there. Samaira has set her sights on becoming president of the United States when she grows up!

Samaira does a lot of public speaking. She's led more than 500 workshops and taught more than 10,000 kids to code. She has spoken about STEM education at more than 100 conferences in the United States and around the world. Samaira also talks to tech workers at big companies like Google, Microsoft, and Intel. Her hope is that her story encourages more girls, and women, to go into engineering. In fact, she actively works with the United Nations to promote **gender equality** in STEM and tech.

At a recent conference in Montréal, Canada, Samaira presented in front of 10,000 people. Then, Google asked her to speak at an event called Take Your Child to Work Day. Google's head of culture, Stacy Sullivan, offered Samaira a job at Google when she gets older. Being offered a job at Google is something most tech people would love.

Samaira thinks coding is a fun superpower, and she wants other kids to feel the same way. She says that coding is the future because the world will depend on it within 10 to 15 years. She wants every kid to think of coding—and being a computer engineer—as a possible job. Samaira dreams of going to college at Stanford University and wants to be an entrepreneur who helps people experiencing homelessness in her community.

EXPLORE MORE! Why not try out one of Samaira's popular games: CoderBunnyz, CoderMindz, or CoderMarz? If you want to learn about coding, check out *Coding for Kids: Python: Learn to Code with 50 Awesome Games and Activities* by Adrienne B. Tacke or *Coding for Kids: Scratch: Learn Coding Skills, Create 10 Fun Games, and Master Scratch* by Matthew Highland.

DID YOU KNOW? Before Samaira created her final version of CoderBunnyz, she first made a prototype, or sample game. She went to libraries to ask if they wanted her to host a workshop to teach kids how to play her game. Lots of them said no, but finally, one said yes. She only had five prototypes when people started asking where they could buy one.

Sophie
CRUZ

2010–present

Sophie Cruz is an American citizen, but her parents, Zoyla and Raul, were born in Mexico and are **undocumented immigrants**. When she was just five years old, Sophie became an activist for Mexican-American immigrants' rights after meeting Pope Francis in Washington, DC.

Sophie Cruz was born on December 17, 2010, in Los Angeles, California. Her parents came to the United States from Oaxaca, Mexico, before Sophie and her sister were born. Sophie's parents came to the United States illegally, and they did not have the right documents to stay in the country. Sophie is very smart. She memorizes poems and reads books way above her grade level. She even skipped kindergarten! Sophie tells her parents, who don't speak very much English, about everything she learns.

Once, Sophie asked if she could go see her grandpa in Mexico. Her parents told Sophie that they could not take her across the border. Because they were in the United States illegally, they probably could not come back to the United States if they left. Sophie wanted to figure out a solution to the problem. She asked her mom where they could buy papers for them to be here legally, but her mother explained that things don't work like that. Sophie decided they needed to fight for the right to stay together. She wanted to help her parents get a green card, which is special permission to stay in the United States.

In 2014, then-President Barack Obama came up with a program called DAPA (Deferred Action for Parents of Americans). DAPA was supposed to help keep families together when parents are immigrants but their children are born in the United States and, therefore, are American citizens. Twenty-six states opposed the plan and brought a case to the Supreme Court to stop it. DAPA was in danger.

When Sophie was just five years old, she went to Washington, DC, to see Pope Francis. He had come in support of undocumented immigrants. Sophie wore a T-shirt that said, in Spanish, *"Papa Rescate DAPA"* (Pope, please save DAPA). She wanted the Pope to support DAPA when he met with leaders in the capital of the United States. Sophie hoped to meet the Pope, give him a note, and ask to speak to him. She did not want her parents to be deported, or sent back, to Mexico.

When the Pope's car drove by, Sophie ran into the street waving at him, but security guards stopped her.

Luckily, the Pope saw Sophie. He waved at her and asked her to come over to him. Then, he gave her a hug, as crowds cheered. Sophie gave him the note she had written. The very next day, Pope Francis met with the US Congress. He brought up the issue of undocumented parents with American children. He asked for leaders to give immigrants and refugees more of a chance to stay with their children who were born in the United States.

Sophie's trip to meet the Pope was paid for by *La Hermandad Mexicana Transnacional* (the Transnational Mexican Sisterhood), an organization based in Los Angeles that fights for immigrants' rights. Sophie's note to Pope Francis said, "Every day I am scared that one day they will take them away from me. I believe I have the right to live with my parents. I have the right to be happy. My dad works very hard. . . . All immigrants just like my dad feed this country. They deserve to live with dignity. They deserve to live with respect." Sophie got lots of media attention from meeting the Pope. She was asking him to help not only her parents, but also the 11 million other undocumented immigrants in the United States.

> ## "I ALSO WANT TO TELL THE CHILDREN NOT TO BE AFRAID, BECAUSE WE ARE NOT ALONE."

In December 2015, Sophie starred in a video about what it would be like for the 4.5 million children of undocumented parents if they were deported. It is heartbreaking and scary for Sophie and her parents to think about so many families being separated by deportation.

In May 2016, Sophie was invited by President Obama to the White House as a "champion of immigration reform." Washington, DC, was having a Cinco de Mayo celebration. Since Sophie's parents didn't have green cards, they could not come with her to the White House. They had to wait at a restaurant nearby. Alida Garcia, a person from an organization that helps immigrants, and Paola Mendoza, a filmmaker who made a video about Sophie and her family, called *Free Like the Birds*, took Sophie to the White House. Her mother said that it broke her heart to miss seeing her daughter meet the president.

On January 21, 2017, six-year-old Sophie spoke to a crowd of tens of thousands at the Women's March on Washington to protest against Donald Trump becoming president. She delivered her speech in English and Spanish. She opened her speech with a positive message, "We are here together, making a chain of love to protect our families. Let us fight with love, faith, and courage so that our families will not be destroyed."

Some people said that adults were telling Sophie what to say so that she could be on the news. Sophie's parents say that all of the ideas come from her. Sophie's father said that his daughter decided to speak out because she is afraid that her parents might get deported. "She understands the reality of what could happen to us," he said. While she and her family do work and coordinate with some nonprofit organizations, nobody is making Sophie speak out.

The Supreme Court ruled against DAPA in 2017, so there is currently no protection for undocumented parents with children who were born in the United States. Sophie still worries that her parents will be deported to Mexico. Sophie is a strong girl and continues to fight for the rights of her parents and millions of other undocumented immigrants.

EXPLORE MORE! Read more about immigrant kids in *America Border Culture Dreamer* by Wendy Ewald. You can also check out the documentary *Free Like the Birds* about Sophie's family. Look for it on the internet.

DID YOU KNOW? Sophie is not only a fighter for immigrants' rights. She also trains in tae kwon do, a martial art like karate, where she learns respect, discipline, and how to defend herself. Sophie says that she has a lot of energy and tae kwon do helps her get that energy out in a positive way.

Glossary

activist: A person who works to bring about change for something they care very much about

artificial intelligence (AI): The ability of a machine to think on its own and learn without a person programming it to do so

autism: A broad range of conditions that show up as challenges with social skills, repeating behaviors or words, speech, and nonverbal communication

boycott: When people stop supporting a company by not buying its products or using its services as a way of protesting

cameo: A small role in a movie played by a very famous person

carbon footprint: The total amount of greenhouse gas (carbon dioxide) each person releases into the air by their actions (like driving a car or heating a home)

chemotherapy: A treatment for cancer using drugs and chemicals

civil rights: Basic rights that every person has under the laws of government to be treated fairly and equally

clinical trials: When scientists and doctors try out a drug to see if it is safe and effective

coder: Someone who writes in computer language to program, or tell, a machine what to do

desegregate: To end laws, policies, or both that keep races apart

diaspora: A group of people who are driven from their homeland to live somewhere else

engineer: A person who builds, designs, or maintains engines, machines, or computers

entrepreneur: Someone who starts their own business from scratch and runs it

gender equality: When people are treated fairly and have equal rights regardless of whether they identify as male, female, or another gender

goodwill ambassador: An honorary title and job given to someone who works for a special cause or global issue—usually a famous person or an expert

immigrant: A person born in one country who moves to another country and settles there

inauguration: When someone is admitted into public office, like the presidency

Indigenous: People who are native to a particular area or region

literary: Having to do with books and reading

loyalty: To be true, or faithful, to someone

nonprofit: An organization that does not make a profit

pen name: The name an author uses for their books, instead of their legal name

poet laureate: A poet who is chosen to represent a country, region, or group

radiation: A treatment for cancer using beams of strong energy to kill cancer cells

rare: Something not often found

refugee: Someone who leaves their homeland to escape danger

rival: An enemy or opponent

royalty: A payment or sum of money

screenplay: A movie script, including acting instructions and scene directions

segregation: The separation of people, usually based on their race or skin color

speech impediment: Having a hard time pronouncing letters or words

stem cell transplant: Removing cells from bone marrow, blood, or umbilical cord blood and putting them into a sick person to give them normal blood cells

tumors: Cancerous growths or swellings caused by abnormal tissue

unconstitutional: Something that does not follow the laws or rules of a country

undocumented immigrant: A person born in another country who comes to a new country without having the necessary documents to live there legally

References

Alex's Lemonade Stand. "Meet our Founder: Alexandra Scott." Accessed February 22, 2022. alexslemonade .org/about/meet-alex.

Austin Film Society. "S.E. Hinton: The Original YA Rebel, and Rumble Fish." Accessed February 22, 2022. austinfilm.org/2016/07/s-e-hinton-the -original-ya-rebel-and-rumble-fish

The Canadian Encyclopedia. "Autumn Peltier." Accessed February 18, 2022. thecanadianencyclopedia.ca/en/article /autumn-peltier.

Burk, Rachelle. *The Story of Simone Biles: A Biography Book for New Readers*. Emeryville, CA: Rockridge Press, 2020.

Cheng, Cynthia. "Santa Clara Resident Samaira Mehta Introduces Game about Artificial Intelligence." *The Silicon Valley Voice*. April 7, 2019. Accessed May 18, 2021. SVVoice.com/santa-clara-resident-samaira -mehta-introduces-game-about-artificial -intelligence.

CBC Kids' News. "On National Child Day, Meet Clean Water Activist Autumn Peltier." Accessed February 22, 2022. youtube.com/watch?v =A33XRMLBbOc.

CBS This Morning. "Teen activist Marley Dias on her new mission for racial harmony." Accessed February 11, 2022. youtube.com/watch?v=sFCrU8j _lu4&feature=emb_imp_woyt.

CNBC. "Amanda Gorman's Inaugural Poem: The Hill We Climb, Full Text." Accessed March 3, 2022. cnbc.com/2021/01/20/amanda-gormans-inaugural -poem-the-hill-we-climb-full-text.html.

Dias, Marley. Accessed February 22, 2022. marleydias.com/about.

Feng, Anna. "My Hero: Alexandra Scott." Accessed February 22, 2022. myhero.com/alexandra-scott-4.

Galat, Joan Marie. *The Story of Malala Yousafzai: A Biography Book for New Readers*. Emeryville, CA: Rockridge Press, 2020.

Girls-Can-Do.org. "About Girls Can Do." Accessed April 14, 2022. Girls-Can-Do.org/about-gcd.

Gorman, Amanda. Accessed March 25, 2022. theamandagorman.com.

Krischer, Hayley. "Why 'The Outsiders' Lives On:
A Teenage Novel Turns 50." *The New York Times.*
March 12, 2017. NYTimes.com/2017/03/12/books
/the-outsiders-s-e-hinton-book.html.

Mukhi, Pranav. "8 Questions for Autumn Peltier. "
Time for Kids. Accessed February 21, 2022.
timeforkids.com/g56/8-questions-for-autumn
-peltier-2.

Neilsen, Euell A. "Black Past: Amanda Gorman."
Accessed March 3, 2022. blackpast.org/african
-american-history/people-african-american
-history/amanda-s-c-gorman-1998.

North American Association for Environmental
Education. "Autumn Peltier." Accessed February 18,
2022. naaee.org/about-us/people/autumn-peltier.

Oklahoma Historical Society. "S. E. Hinton." Accessed
February 22, 2022. okhistory.org/publications/enc
/entry.php?entry=HI013.

Park West Gallery. "Inside the Artist's Studio: Autumn
de Forest." November 9, 2016. Accessed June 9, 2021.
Youtube.com/watch?v=4fM9t2RKaGg.

Part, Michael. *The Greta Thunberg Story: Being
Different Is a Superpower.* Beverly Hills, CA: Sole
Books, 2019.

Paumgarten, Nick. "The Wall Dancer: Ashima Shiraishi's Route to the Top." *The New Yorker*. January 3, 2016. NewYorker.com/magazine/2016/01/11/the-wall-dancer.

PBS Learning Media. "Audrey Hendricks." 2004. Accessed May 20, 2021. CA.PBSLearningMedia.org/resource/iml04.soc.ush.civil.ahendric/audrey-hendricks.

Rothberg, Emma. "Audrey Faye Hendricks." National Women's History Museum. 2020. Accessed May 20, 2021. WomensHistory.org/education-resources/biographies/audrey-faye-hendricks.

S. E. Hinton. Accessed February 22, 2022. sehinton.com/bioframe.html.

Silva, Daniella. "'We're Human, Too': Simone Biles Highlights Importance of Mental Health in Olympics Withdrawal." NBC Universal News Group. July 27, 2021. Last updated July 28, 2021. NBCNews.com/news/olympics/we-re-human-too-simone-biles-highlights-importance-mental-health-n1275224.

"The Original Alex Scott Documentary." Accessed February 25, 2022. youtube.com/watch?v=6d2QOmQOP4U.

Thunberg, Greta. *No One Is Too Small to Make a Difference*. New York: Penguin, 2019.

Whiting, Sam. "Yuan Yuan Tan Goes On and On, Extending Her Ballet Record for Longevity." *San Francisco Chronicle DATEBOOK*. January 7, 2020. Last updated January 8, 2020. DATEBOOK .SFChronicle.com/dance/yuan-yuan-tan-goes-on -and-on-extending-her-ballet-record-for-longevity.

Young, Henry. "Yusra Mardini: 'I represent more than Syria, I represent millions around the world.'" CNN. May 10, 2018. CNN.com/2018/05/09/sport/yusra -mardini-syrian-swimmer-rio-2016-olympics-spt /index.html.

Acknowledgments

First and foremost, I appreciate my outstanding editor, Barbara, who entrusted me with this book and guided me with grace, precision, and determination. I appreciate my parents, Janice and Ray, for their encouragement. To my brother, Steve, thanks! Kudos to my talented writers' group—Andrew, Brandi, Chris, Evan, Jasmine, and Sonia. In memory of my Grandma Grace, my Aunt Judy, and my mentors, Ilse and Bill. To my nephews Sam, Jacob, and David, and my nieces Sofia and Katherine. Thanks to the entire Callisto team, including Ariel, who helped me market the books! I am supported by family and friends: Michelle G., Susan, Ann & Greg, Jeanne, Deborah, Kiernan, Laurie, Tanya, Carla, Julia & Ira, Maureen, Amparo, Michael, Ricardo, Alejandra, Arden, Jen, Tami, Karen, Annie, Crystal, Bryan, Jessica, Marji, Marcy, Lara, Anita & Bob, Jerry, Nena & Mel, Jami, Stacy & Rick, Laura & Darren, Michelle R., Chalmers, Violeta, Diana y Juanca, and Sylvia Boorstein. Special thanks to our incredible sensitivity readers.

About the Author

Susan B. Katz is an award-winning, bestselling, bilingual author; National Board certified teacher; educational consultant; and keynote speaker. Susan has more than 30 published books, and 18 forthcoming, with Scholastic, Random House, Simon & Schuster, Callisto/Rockridge, and Barefoot Books. When she's not writing, Susan enjoys traveling, snorkeling, wildlife photography, salsa dancing, and spending time at the beach. You can find out more about her books and school visits at SusanKatzBooks.com and see her photography at Behance.net/susanbkatz.

About the Illustrator

Monika Róża Wiśniewska is an illustrator from Poland, working with publishers all over the world. In 2017 she graduated with a master of arts from the Nicolaus Copernicus University in Toruń, Poland. Since 2020, she's been working with Advocate Art. You can see her work on her website MonikaRoza.com.